To My Sisters Beloved

A Trilogy of Encouragement

Bishop Timothy J. Clarke

Forward by
Mrs. Clytemnestra L. Clarke

To My Sisters Beloved: A Trilogy of Encouragement ©2011 by Timothy J. Clarke

Scripture references noted "KJV" are taken from the Holy Bible, King James Version. Public domain.

Scripture references noted "NIV" are taken from the Holy Bible, New International Version, copyright © 1973, 1978, 1984 by International Bible Society. Used by permission of Zondervan Bible Publishers. All rights reserved.

Scripture references noted "NLT" are taken from the Holy Bible, New Living Translation, copyright © 1996. Used by permission of Tyndale House Publishers, Inc., Wheaton, Illinois 60189. All rights reserved.

Scriptures references noted "MSG" are taken from The Message. Copyright © 1993, 1994, 1995, 1996, 2000, 2001, 2002. Used by permission of NavPress Publishing Group. All rights reserved.

Daughter Don't Miss Your Season
Copyright©2002 by Timothy J. Clarke, First Edition
Copyright©2011 by Timothy J. Clarke, Revised Edition

Hannah Rose, Copyright©2004 by Timothy J. Clarke
Copyright©2011 by Timothy J. Clarke, First Edition

Help For Those Who Hurt
Copyright©2002 by Timothy J. Clarke, First Edition
Copyright©2011 by Timothy J. Clarke, Revised Edition

Powerful Purpose Publishing
P O Box 32132
Columbus, OH 43232

Publishing Consultant: Obieray Rogers (www.rubiopublishing.com)

ISBN 978-0-9764022-6-8

Printed in the United States of America

Dedicated to the women of

God everywhere.

Foreword

Only time and eternity will reveal my level of appreciation to God for allowing me to be the life partner of Bishop Timothy Joseph Clarke. It has been an incredible journey and I had no idea of the blessings I would receive as I came along for the ride. His love and support has been a constant in my life and has shown me how to better love, serve, and minister to others. For almost thirty-five years now, I have had the privilege of sitting under one of the most dynamic and anointed preachers of the gospel. I can truly say that my life has been blessed, inspired, encouraged, enriched, enhanced, and edified by the ministry and leadership of Bishop.

It is no secret that Bishop is known for his preaching and teaching gifts and abilities, and in recent years, it has been my joy to watch God use him to bring help, healing, hope, and encouragement in the written form. If you have had the opportunity to read any of the numerous books that Bishop has penned, you will attest to the fact that they have impacted your life in a positive and significant way. This latest trilogy is a compilation of some of his best work that has been especially designed to minister to women of all ages and experiences. Each book looks at and addresses the unique needs of women through practical and encouraging instructions.

Whether your past, your predicament, or your perception is hindering you from fulfilling your destiny; or you are living with contradiction and needing to rise up out of the ashes of despair and discouragement; or you are experiencing deep emotional hurt and need a word of hope, you will find that this trilogy will minister to the very place of your need. Throughout these written pages you will discover that Bishop has shared straight from his pastor's heart that is full of care, compassion, and concern.

Life and time both have a way of helping us to acknowledge, appreciate, and value those who God uses to help and bless us along our journey. I believe you will appreciate and value the time and work of our author and will thank God for his insight and wisdom as you are enlightened and enriched by the message of hope.

So my beloved sister, my prayer is that this book will be a great source of comfort and encouragement as you continue on the path to spiritual growth and development. Grace and Peace!

Lady "C"

Daughter

Don't Miss Your Season!

This book is dedicated to the first women
God put in my life:

My mother ~ Essie Bailey

My grandmother ~ Josephine Bailey

My aunts ~ Betty and Bertha

My sisters ~ Josephine and Jackie

I miss love, and remember you all.

Table of Contents

Introduction

After preaching for over thirty-five years, I am aware there are times the Lord gives me a specific message for a specific group of people. This book is one such message.

I sense in my spirit that God is about to take His women to a place that will literally be the beginning of a new season for them. The thing you must fight and persevere against is to not allow anything or anyone to cause you to miss your season.

Your season is so important that whomever you have to get rid of, you must be willing to let them go.

Your season is so important that whatever changes you have to make, you must be willing to make them.

Your season is so important that whatever you have to do (or stop doing), you must be willing to make the change.

The story of Naomi is just one of many examples in the Bible of people operating in their season. She has much to teach you about walking in your season.

Naomi Represents Every Woman

In order for you to appreciate what I am going to share, you must understand the pilgrimage of the woman whose life we are examining.

The Holy Spirit showed me that Naomi represents every woman because every woman has been a Naomi at some point in her life. The book of Ruth opens with Naomi as a young woman, newly married, and having the time of her life. Everything is going well. That is where some of you are. You're in the spring of your life where everything is new and fresh. You have a husband, the house with a white picket fence, a job, career, degree, and money to get your hair and nails done every week. Your life is just wonderful.

Ruth chapter one opens with Naomi as a wife and mother and the envy of other women. Her husband loves her and her children adore her, but then things change. There is a famine in the land and her husband loses his job and all of a sudden

Naomi has to get her hair done on somebody's back porch instead of at the beauty salon. She no longer has money to do what she used to do. Because of the famine, Elimelech uproots his family and moves them to a foreign land:

> *In the days when the judges ruled, there was a famine in the land, and a man from Bethlehem in Judah, together with his wife and two sons, went to live for a while in the country of Moab.* (Ruth 1:1, NIV)

And then things changed again:

> *Now Elimelech, Naomi's husband, died and she was left with her two sons. They married Moabite women, one named Orpah and the other Ruth. After they had lived there about ten years, both Mahlon and Kilion also died, and Naomi was left without her two sons and her husband.* (Ruth 1:3-5, NIV)

Isn't it interesting how you can leave home in the morning, kiss your husband goodbye, and think you have a perfect marriage? Then you return home to discover that your husband has left you a note telling you thanks for the memories, and in less than twenty-four hours your perfect world is turned upside down. At six in the morning you're on top of the world; by six in the evening the world is on top of you!

Naomi is a woman who knows love and loss, pain and grief. Can you relate to her yet? Here is a woman who has seen it all. Naomi is every woman, whether a seasoned mother or a young saint just coming to know the Lord. She is the young woman with her future before her, planning with her husband their first child, and the older woman looking back and wondering if life has not passed her by.

YOU ARE A SURVIVOR!

What I like about Naomi is that in spite of all she has been through, she is a survivor. And so are you. You may not have your story in the Bible or the local newspaper, but you are a survivor. You have been to hell and back. You have cried, you have experienced loss, you have struggled and fell. You have had your heart broken. You have been mistreated, played, and jerked around by life and men. You have been hurt by your parents, siblings, and false friends. They thought it was going to take you out or pull you down, but here you are. You have scars and pain, but you made it. You are a survivor!

If you read chapter one with any kind of sanctified imagination, you will discover that Naomi went through hell. She lost her husband and both sons in a foreign land. She grew old and lived in a culture where women were devalued. Yet, she survived. There isn't a woman who can't identify with Naomi because she reminds you that whatever you do, don't miss your season.

GOD HAS KEPT YOU ALIVE

I know some of you believe you have missed your season and it's all over, but it isn't. As long as you are breathing, you have not missed your next season. Your season is what the Lord births you for and where the Lord is taking you. It is so important that you understand the time and seasons of your life. It is also important that whatever you do, you don't miss your season:

> *So Naomi returned from Moab accompanied by Ruth the Moabitess, her daughter-in-law,*

arriving in Bethlehem as the barley harvest was beginning. (Ruth 1:22, NIV)

You may have missed a previous season, but as long as you're still alive, you qualify to make it to the next one. You don't qualify because of your age or because you have done everything right. You don't qualify because you have been some wonderful, fabulous, fantastic, perfect, dotted-every-I-crossed-every-T-and-resisted-every-temptation person. It isn't because you didn't return his phone call, or take him up on his offer, or string some man along, or gave up a little bit to get a little bit. That is not why you are qualified. All of us have skeletons in our closets and some of them still have meat on them. All of us have failed, fallen, been tempted, *and* yielded. No, you don't qualify because you have been perfect. You qualify because God has kept you alive. And since God has kept you alive, He did so for a reason and a purpose.

What Is A Season?

$\mathscr{I}$asked the Lord "What is a season?" and He said a season is the period of time when you are the most fruitful and productive.

When you're in your season, you don't have to work nearly as hard as when you're not. When you're in your season, you don't even have to strain because things begin to flow. As a matter of fact, one of the ways you will know you're in your season is that things start getting easier. You almost get to the point where you look at things and people and just smile because you want to say, "Just save the drama." You get to a point where you watch foolishness and three days ago it would have upset you, a week ago it would have gotten on your last nerve, a month ago you would have been having a fit. Now you look at people and smile and then do what you have to do. When you're in your season, you don't have to push, pull, or tug because your season propels you with a power that is greater than yourself. You're flowing in the divine activity of God. A season is a period of time when you're fruitful and optimum in your productivity.

A season is a cycle. As a woman you know what your cycle does. At certain times of the month you are fertile. Fertile is just another word for fruitful, a time when you are able to bring something forth. After ovulation, if nothing is seeded, you then begin your cycle, which pushes out the impurities and the dead stuff that prepares you for another cycle. My sister, God created you in such a way that if during your ovulation no semen impregnates you, it doesn't stay there. All of the dead stuff is purged out to get you ready for another cycle. The pain, pressure, and discomfort you are feeling is merely God purging some dead stuff out of you.

When you're in your season, you're fertile and ready to produce. That is why you can't miss your season, because you don't know what God is wanting to birth and produce in you during this time.

What Hinders Our Season?

Let's take a look at some of the elements that will make you miss your season.

YOUR PAST

Everybody has a past. I don't know why you trip when people get saved who talk about how they used to live. Maybe they have been married three or four times, or have been shacking up with somebody, or they had a child out of wedlock. You want to sit around with your arms across your bosom with a holier-than-thou look on your face as if to say, "My God, what is the church coming to. I mean, if this is the kind of folks we're getting." First of all, help me understand what kind of folks should we be getting? I'm really confused. You seem surprised and upset when adulterers, whoremongers, pimps, pushers, drug addicts, homosexuals, and lesbians come to the Lord. You want to get mad and go on a witch hunt and dig up their past because you are not sure if you want *those* kind of folks in your church. But, wait one minute, what kind of folks do you want? Who are we preaching to if we are not preaching to sinners? The only folks who need to be saved are sinners!

One of the tricks the devil will use to intimidate you is your past. The reason you're not operating in your gift isn't fear, but intimidation. The devil and the ain'ts (not the saints) got their bluff in before the game started and you haven't gone onto the field yet. You let them scare you into inaction. They look at you funny as if they know something. Some of them just might, but you need to remember (and then remind them) that whatever they know about your past is just that. . .your past.

The good news is that God is not holding your past against you. God is not holding that marriage against you; that abortion against you; that child out of wedlock against you; that excursion into drug addiction against you. Perhaps you're squeaky clean and have never done anything, so go find somebody and tell them I said that God is not holding their past against them: "*As far as the east is from the west, so far hath he removed our transgressions from us"* (Psalm 103:12, KJV).

You can't let your past keep you from your season. I want to liberate women to stop sitting in church afraid and intimidated because of your past. That is why you're not flowing in your gift. Some of you are so highly anointed, yet you have been intimidated by the enemy, the devil, and the ain'ts and you're sitting on your gift. Don't let your past keep you from your season.

The first chapter of Ruth is so pregnant with truth. Naomi lost her husband and sons, so why didn't she give up and die? With all of her pain, hurt, and suffering, why didn't she just curl up in a fetal position, suck her thumb and die? I think Naomi understood she couldn't let her past keep her from her season.

YOUR PREDICAMENT

If your past is where you have been, then your predicament is where you are now. Naomi teaches us a lot about handling predicaments. First of all, she is old and that is a predicament. She is alone and

19

that is a predicament. And she is a woman in a male dominated culture and that is really a predicament:

> *But on the way, Naomi said to her two daughters-in-law, "Go back to your mothers' homes. And may the LORD reward you for your kindness to your husbands and to me. May the LORD bless you with the security of another marriage." Then she kissed them good-bye, and they all broke down and wept. "No," they said. "We want to go with you to your people." But Naomi replied, "Why should you go on with me? Can I still give birth to other sons who could grow up to be your husbands? No, my daughters, return to your parents' homes, for I am too old to marry again. And even if it were possible, and I were to get married tonight and bear sons, then what? Would you wait for them to grow up and refuse to marry someone else? No, of course not, my daughters! Things are far more bitter for me than for you, because the LORD himself has raised his fist against me."* (Ruth 1:8-13, NLT)

Some of you are in a messy marriage and that is your predicament. You are trying to live a saved life with an unsaved heathen for a husband. Some of you have nice unsaved husbands and some of you are married to Lucifer's second cousin. He is as mean as a rattlesnake and twice as ugly and that is a predicament. Some of you are on a dead-end job and that is a predicament. Some of your children are rebellious and that is a predicament. Others of you have a financial challenge and that is a predicament. Let's be honest, some of you created the predicament you're in, but it's still a predicament nonetheless.

I don't care how they look on the outside, every woman has a predicament of some kind, so stop player hating on your sisters! One of the most effective tools the enemy has used is catty women. There isn't anything worse than a woman giving a compliment with an edge to it, because they cut you and you don't really know you're bleeding until you look down. "You look very nice . . . today." Forget everything except the word "today." Instead of ministering, encouraging, praying, and exhorting one another, you're player hating because the sister comes to church with her hair and clothes looking nice and you think, "Who does she think she is? She is always trying to show somebody up." You have no idea what is going on with her. The only way she is making it is by getting dressed, putting on makeup, and saying to herself, "I'm not giving in to the devil. I'm not going out like this. I'm going to walk in there with my head held high even though my heart is breaking and my life is out of control. I'm still going to walk in there like everything is all right."

If you could spend time with the sister that you talked about just last Sunday, you would be surprised. She walks in with her husband and they appear to be Mr. and Mrs. Perfect. You don't know that he uses her for a punching bag. You don't know that they are about to get a divorce. You don't know that she just found out he has cheated on her for the fifth time. You don't know that she was just diagnosed with breast cancer. You don't know that her husband has prostate cancer. You're player hating on them and their world is about to spiral out of control. Every woman has her own private predicament, which is why you have to encourage, exalt, love, pray, and support one another.

Your predicament is where you are now. It is the thing you struggle with. It is the thing you are trying to get on top of. You try to wrestle with it and handle it. You try to master it, and just when you think you have it under control, it will flip you. It's a predicament.

YOUR PERCEPTION

Naomi did good dealing with her past. She didn't give up and die; she handled her past. She didn't let her predicament keep her from her season. But you know what almost kept her back? Her perception. Here is where Naomi missed it, which only goes to show that nobody is perfect:

Naomi told Ruth and Orpah:

> *"No, my daughters, return to your parents' homes, for I am too old to marry again. And even if it were possible, and I were to get married tonight and bear sons, then what?"*
> (Ruth 1:12, NLT)

23

Then Naomi told them:

> *"Would you wait for them to grow up and refuse to marry someone else? No, of course not, my daughters! Things are far more bitter for me than for you, because the LORD himself has raised his fist against me."* (Ruth 1:13, NLT)

And then Naomi really lost touch with reality:

> *So the two of them continued on their journey. When they came to Bethlehem, the entire town was excited by their arrival. "Is it really Naomi?" the women asked. "Don't call me Naomi," she responded. "Instead, call me Mara, for the Almighty has made life very bitter for me. I went away full, but the LORD has brought me home empty. Why call me Naomi when the LORD has caused me to suffer and the Almighty has sent such tragedy upon me?"* (Ruth 1:19-21, NLT)

Nothing can keep you from your season like a messed up perception when you let the devil convince you that people, the saints, your pastor, and even God is against you. Some of you have asked God in your private moments, "What's wrong with me?" "Why is everybody else getting married?" "Why is everybody else getting blessed?" "Why is everybody else prospering?" "Why is everybody else flowing?" "Why is everybody else getting everything they want?" "Why are you against me?"

If you don't change your perception, you're going to start getting bitter and angry with God, which is something you don't want to do. You never want to fight God because you want Him on your side. You need to understand that you are always beloved and precious in His eyes. No matter what is going on in your life, God loves you!

You must change your perception and stop talking negative: "I'm overweight, who wants me?" "I'm the wrong color, who wants me?" "I'm old, who wants me?" Stand naked in a full-length mirror; turn around, look at yourself from every angle and say, "Even in this present shape, God still loves me." Learn how to encourage yourself. Find something about you that you like if it isn't anything but the shape of your toes. Look at your feet and say, "I started at my head and couldn't find anything until I got to my toes. Look at the angle of my toes. Look at

how they curve. Look at how symmetrical they are."
You have to love them and realize that God spent
extra time making your toes because he loves you
that much!

If you don't change your perception, you're
never going to get to your season because you will
have convinced yourself you don't deserve one.
There are so many women who have convinced
themselves they don't deserve any better and that is
why they keep getting what they get. You wonder
why you have been a magnet for nuts. You're like
flypaper; you draw, attract, and keep crazy, broke,
non-working, and no good men. You know why?
Because you send out vibes that this is all you
deserve. Every man you have ever been with has
mentally, emotionally, physically, or sexually
abused you because you send a signal that this is all
you deserve. You must change your perception.
Stop downing yourself and start believing in yourself.

*G*od is determined to get you to your season. That is why He has been so patient. That is why He hasn't cut you off in all of your foolishness. That is why He has put up with you with all of your fumbling, bumbling, and inconsistencies. That is why He hasn't wiped you out for continually going back into the same sin that He has delivered you out of thirty-three times before. The only reason He is still putting up with you is because He sees your season and He is trying to get you to the place where you walk in it: *"For I know the plans I have for you,"* says *the Lord. "They are plans for good and not for disaster, to give you a future and a hope."* (Jeremiah 29:11, NLT)

WHAT GOD HAS PUT IN YOU

The seed a farmer plants represents a deposit on his part. What gives the farmer hope and confidence is that he understands the potential of a seed. The seed itself is never big or pretty and no one gets excited about it. Seeds have only one purpose — to be planted — and seeds don't do their job until they are out of sight. What makes a farmer excited is the potential that is in a seed.

Your season represents what God has put in you. There are two times God makes a deposit inside you. The first time is when you're born and He gives you natural talent. Every woman is good at something. The second deposit is when you're born again and He puts a spiritual (or grace) gift inside of you. Both times He has planted a seed in you and your season is when God expects a return on what He has planted:

> *And he shall be like a tree planted by the rivers of water, that bringeth forth his fruit in his season; his leaf also shall not wither; and whatsoever he doeth shall prosper.* (Psalm 1:3, KJV)

You haven't been using your talents or gifts and God told me to tell you that your delivery date is past due! The seed is the potential of what you can become. Do you have any idea what you could

28

really be if you would hook up with God? Do you have any idea the lives you could touch and the difference you could make if you would let God move you into your season? Do you know the people who are not being touched, healed, helped, or ministered to because you're not operating in your season? Do you know how many churches are not functioning as they should or the children who aren't being taught simply because you're not living up to your potential? There is not a Christian woman alive who hasn't had two deposits made in her life: Talent at birth; a gift at spiritual birth. Here is the question, what are you doing with the seed? Are you cultivating and watering it? You should be because it represents what God has put in you.

WHAT GOD HAS PUT ON YOU

Seeds are planted at certain times of the season. You can plant good seed too late and it won't produce. You have to give the seed time to mature. The farmer either waits on God to send rain or he will water the ground himself. Most of you don't like God's rain. You want blue skies and sunshine all of the time and some of you think that is a sign that you're walking in God's will. You need to remember that nothing grows with just blue skies and sunshine. What God puts on you is as important as what He has put in you.

You like thinking you have seed and potential inside you, but nothing will bring out the potential except adversity and struggle. You need to stop rebuking and binding some stuff because it isn't the devil doing it. There is some stuff that you have been running from that comes from God. There are some painful and difficult things that God puts on you because of what He has put in you.

As a matter of fact, the more He has put in you, the more He is going to put on you. What it takes to grow a mushroom and what it takes to grow an oak tree is all determined by how much rain falls on it. A whole lot of you haven't gone deeper or higher because you keep avoiding the necessary step that God wants to put on you because of what He has already put in you.

You have been wondering, "Why am I going through this now?" "Why is all this happening to me now?" The operative word is "now." If it is happening now, now must be the time. Just be glad God didn't do it yesterday, because you weren't ready. Be glad God didn't do it last week, because you couldn't have handled it. Be glad God didn't do it last year, because you couldn't have stood it. If God is doing it now, He knows that now is the time. Because of what He has put in, you are able to handle what He has put on, and what He has put on is directly related to what He has put in you.

WHAT GOD PRODUCES THROUGH YOU

God never produces through you without putting something on you, and He never puts on you what is not already in you. What He has put inside you determines what He has put on you, and what He puts on you determines what He produces through you.

Some of you need to stop testifying because when you do you let us know that God hasn't put much in you. We are sick of your junk food testimony. We are sick of you talking about how everything is wonderful in your life, because all you're doing is telling us there isn't much in you. If nothing is being put on you, it's because God hasn't put anything in you and isn't expecting much out of you.

When you can testify, "I'm in a strange place." "I'm in a tight place." "I'm in a place I don't understand," then we can start shouting with you. We know if God is putting that much on you, there is no telling what is in you and what is coming out of you. Whatever is coming out has to be mighty because of how much God is putting on you. The end result is going to be great. God never puts more on you than what He expects out of you.

TRANSITIONS

Naomi went from Ruth 1:20-21 (NLT). . .

> *"Don't call me Naomi," she responded. "Instead, call me Mara, for the Almighty has made life very bitter for me. I went away full, but the LORD has brought me home empty. Why call me Naomi when the LORD has caused me to suffer and the Almighty has sent such tragedy upon me?"*

To Ruth 4:16 (NLT). . .

Naomi took the baby and cuddled him to her breast. And she cared for him as if he were her own.

Another word for "cared" is nurse. She is an old woman but she is nursing. I know some of you will say that the word "nurse" in Hebrew means she took care of the baby and you would be absolutely correct; she cared for and babysat the child. But there wasn't any formula back then, so if Naomi nursed her grandson she had to nurse him at her breast. What is an old woman doing with milk in her breasts?

If you hang in there and if you go through the rain and pain, a new season is coming. God will give life where it looks like death. He will give you milk where things look dried up. Even in your old age you can still nurse because your season is promised. Nothing can stop you once you get in your season. You can nurse your business, nurse your career, or nurse your degree. Even in old age God will give you milk.

What's Ahead?

This is the beginning of your season so whatever you do, don't miss it. Don't let your past, your predicament, or your perception keep you from your season.

Your season represents what God has put in you. Have you ever stopped to take inventory of what is in you? Why do you like the things you like? Why do you enjoy doing certain things? You thought it was just a hobby, but maybe it's your seed. We miss seasons because we don't understand them. God has made two deposits into every Christian woman: At birth He gave you talent; at your second birth He gave you a spiritual gift. What are you doing with the seed?

Your season represents what God has put on you. When I realized that, it blessed me because I saw a seed in the ground and torrential rain coming down. The rain is what makes it grow. God has put some stuff on you because of what He has put in you.

Your season represents what God will produce through you. The more He puts on you, the more He will produce through you. Stop running from your challenges. Stop running from your struggles. It's your trials that will make you strong.

Conclusion

The seeds of your destiny, your purpose and your calling are all in you. Everything God wants and expects out of you is already there. God allows the pressure, pain, and problems of life to get out — literally push out — what He has put inside you. What we often see and celebrate about a person is the finished product. What we don't see, and would not appreciate, is the making process. We see the baby, but we don't see the labor or hold the after-birth. What we see now is what was in the person all the time; it just had to be delivered. That means there was ugliness and pain involved, but the end result was worth the struggle.

God has a future for you. I don't care how old you are, you can still nurse. Since you're still alive, that means you haven't missed your season. You may have missed a previous season, but you're just in time for your next one:

So Naomi returned from Moab accompanied by Ruth the Moabitess, her daughter-in-law, arriving in Bethlehem as the barley harvest was beginning. (Ruth 1:22, NIV)

God specific message for you is, *"Daughter, Don't Miss Your Season!"*

Hannah Rose:

Lessons from a desperate woman

Dedication

There are three things I know
I have done right:
First was accepting Christ as my Savior.
Second was saying yes to God's will for my life.
Third was marrying Clytemnestra thirty-five
years ago. This book is dedicated to her.

Table of Contents

Dear Sister,

I have an announcement to make: You are a woman of purpose and destiny who was known by God before you were born. He has created a blueprint for your life, and in spite of what the devil has tried to do to block, hinder, or stop it, the perfect will of God shall prevail. God has given me insight from the story of Hannah to push and propel you into the next dimension for your life: The place where God wants to take you and use you to His glory. This is a Word from God specifically for you.

There comes a time in the life of every woman when she has to be a Hannah. At that moment, she has to make up her mind that no matter what she has been through, no matter what has happened in her life, no matter how much bitterness or suffering or sorrow she has endured and experienced, she will be like Hannah and say, "In spite of where I am, I *am* rising up from here."

Every woman of God has a moment when she cannot allow the things that have happened (or are happening) to hold her back from her destiny and purpose. You are that woman. You have to make up your mind to rise above where you are.

You have to believe that if Hannah could rise, you can rise, too.

I really wish there were more women like Hannah who would say, "I've been through the storm; I've been through the rain, I've been through heartache and pain, but the fact that I'm still here says I have enough strength to get up from here." You don't have to stay down. You don't have to stay defeated. And you don't have to stay in a place of despair and depression.

Life is filled with those things that will steal our joy if we're not careful. I call them joy busters:

- Fear is a joy buster. Someone has said that fear is false evidence appearing real. When we allow fear to enter our lives, it can immobilize us and cause us to become stuck in our past and our pain. Stuck people never move, grow, or advance. They are stuck; so they stay where and like they are.

- Frustration is also a joy buster. All of us know the draining, depleting nature of frustration. We can get frustrated at our lack of progress or the constancy of the struggle.

Sometimes we get frustrated with the process itself. Frustration is like a blanket; it can smother us or extinguish the fire that is within us.

- Fatigue is yet another joy buster. Sometimes we just get tired and feel like giving up. Fatigue is real and takes its toll on us. This is an area we often overlook and neglect. We have to take care of ourselves.

Fear, frustration, and fatigue are just a few of the joy busters we are confronted with and we have to guard and fight against these culprits on a regular basis. This fight takes place on several levels:

- Spiritually by staying grounded in the disciplines of prayer, Bible study, fasting, meditation, and worship (both corporate and private).

- Physically by getting enough rest, taking Sabbaths, and exercising our bodies.

47

- Emotionally by guarding our hearts and setting a watch at the door of our minds.

I wrote *Hannah Rose: Lessons from a desperate woman* to declare to you that your sad days are over. The joy of the Lord is your strength. You may not have a man, but you have joy. You may not have a job, but you have joy. You may not have everything you have been asking for, but you have joy. Joy is the secret weapon to get you to where you have to go. If you can hold onto your joy, there is nothing the devil can do to you.

I believe that God has given me a Word for you. I pray that by the end of this book you will have made a life-changing decision that will propel you further into your destiny, but you're not going to get there until you're willing to make a change.

1 Samuel 1:1-19, MSG

There once was a man who lived in Ramathaim. He was descended from the old Zuph family in the Ephraim hills. His name was Elkanah. (He was connected with the Zuphs from Ephraim through his father Jeroham, his grandfather Elihu and his great-grandfather Tohu). He had two wives. The first was Hannah; the second was Peninnah. Peninnah had children; Hannah did not.

Every year this man went from his hometown up to Shiloh to worship and offer a sacrifice to God-of-the-Angel-Armies. Eli and his two sons, Hophni and Phinehas, served as the priests of God there. When Elkanah sacrificed, he passed helpings from the sacrificial meal around to his wife Peninnah and all her children, but he always gave an especially generous helping to Hannah because he loved her so much, and because God had not given her children. But her rival wife taunted her cruelly, rubbing it in and never letting her forget that God had not given her children. This went on year after year. Every time she went to the sanctuary of God she could expect to be taunted. Hannah was reduced to tears and had no appetite.

Her husband Elkanah said, "Oh, Hannah, why are you crying? Why aren't you eating? And why are you so upset? Am I not of more worth to you than ten sons?"

*So Hannah ate. Then she pulled herself together,
slipped away quietly and entered the sanctuary. The priest Eli
was on duty at the entrance to God's Temple in the customary
seat. Crushed in spirit, Hannah prayed to God and cried and
cried — inconsolably. Then she made a vow: Oh, God-of-the-
Angels-Armies, if you'll take a good, hard look at my pain, if
you'll quit neglecting me and go into action for me by giving
me a son, I'll give him completely, unreservedly to you. I'll set
him apart for a life of holy discipline.*

*It so happened that as she continued in prayer before
God, Eli was watching her closely. Hannah was praying in her
heart, silently. Her lips moved, but no sound was heard. Eli
jumped to the conclusion that she was drunk. He approached
her and said, "You're drunk! How long do you plan to keep
this up? Sober up, woman!"*

*Hannah said, "Oh no, sir — please! I'm a woman hard
used. I haven't been drinking. Not a drop of wine or beer. The
only thing I've been pouring out is my heart, pouring it out to
God. Don't for a minute think I'm a bad woman. It's because
I'm so desperately unhappy and in such pain that I've stayed
here so long."*

*Eli answered her, "Go in peace. And may the God of
Israel give you what you have asked of him."*

*"Think well of me — and pray for me!" she said, and
went her way. Then she ate heartily, her face radiant.*

*Up before dawn, they worshipped God and returned
home to Ramah. Elkanah slept with Hannah his wife, and God
began making the necessary arrangements in response to what
she had asked.*

Chapter One
Rise Up, Move On, and Go Higher

———————

One of the problems some women have is that they have been in a situation or a relationship too long. God never planned for you to be on that job twenty years. The job was meant to be temporary until your destiny kicked in. You're about to abort your destiny on a dead-end job, but I'm anointed to get you out of every dead-end situation, relationship, and job.

You've been dating that man for seven years and he hasn't given you an engagement ring yet! Today, you're going to help him pack his bags and tell him to hit the road. He has had seven years — the number of completion — and you're turning him out and rising up and moving into your destiny.

Some of you have been with a person too long and it is not just a man. Some of you have girlfriends you need to cut loose: dead-end-negative-blood-sucking-life-taking-joy-draining-money-borrowing-and-never-pay-you-back-player-hating-trying-to-steal-your-man-when-you're-not-around-girlfriends, and you're still trying to hold onto them! You can cut the cord and get rid of every bloodsucker in your life.

> *There was a certain man from Ramathaim, a Zuphite from the hill country of Ephraim, whose name was Elkanah son of Jeroham, the son of Elihu, the son of Tohu, the son of Zuph, an Ephraimite. He had two wives; one was called Hannah and the other Peninnah. Peninnah had children, but Hannah had none.* (1 Samuel 1:1-2, NIV)

When we are first introduced to Hannah, she is immediately identified as a barren woman, which was causing her great pain and had her stuck in a rut. It doesn't matter who you are; every woman lives with deficiencies. I know you think other women have it going on, but if you only knew the truth you would realize that things are not as they seem. I know you think that because they have a husband, a job, live in a nice house and have nice clothes that they live in a perfect world, but if you only knew what went on behind closed doors, you would be amazed. Everything that glitters isn't gold. Every woman has something that represents a deficiency in her life.

Hannah had a problem: She was barren. That didn't make her unique because she wasn't the only barren woman nor was she the only woman with a problem. Her challenge was that she allowed her problem to get her stuck. It's easy to get stuck. Sometimes it even feels good to be stuck. We start getting used to where we are (physically, emotionally, and professionally) and then we get comfortable. We are acquainted and familiar with where we are and, frankly, it takes too must effort to change. Staying where you are is more costly and painful than going where God has destined you. Let me tell you why. If you stay stuck, you will eventually succumb. In other words, you will die where you are and the tragedy is that you will then miss all that God has for you.

William Shakespeare wrote, "Cowards die many times before their deaths. The valiant never taste of death but once." The same is true of women who get stuck in their pain, past, and predicament. They, too, die a thousand little painful deaths and never grasp what God has for them. How do you avoid this?

- By developing your faith (that earnest hope and expectation).
- By staying focused (maintaining a clear commitment to what you want).
- By building up your fortitude (staying diligent).

If you're stuck, the good news is that you can become unstuck once you make up your mind that, like Hannah, you're getting up from where you are.

Chapter Two
Contending or Contentment:
Living with a Contradiction

─────────────────────────────────────

I realize that what you're about to read could be argued two ways: Hannah should have been happy with her husband and his love. She had a husband who loved her, but her womb was shut up. On the one hand it is good, but on the other hand it's like, "What have I done to deserve this?" But here is a powerful principal to remember: Life is never all good or all bad. It has ebbs and flows; peaks and valleys, seasons:

> *Year after year this man went up from his town to worship and sacrifice to the Lord Almighty at Shiloh, where Hophni and Phinehas, the two sons of Eli, were priests of the Lord. Whenever the day came for Elkanah to sacrifice, he would give portions of the meat*

to his wife Peninnah and to all her sons and daughters. But to Hannah he gave a double portion because he loved her, and the Lord had closed her womb. (1 Samuel 1:3-5, NIV)

There is a part of this argument where one could say that Hannah should have been content with the love of her husband who took very good care of her. Hannah received a double portion of everything. If Elkanah brought Peninnah one dress, he bought Hannah two. If he bought Peninnah one pair of shoes, he brought Hannah two. If he gave Peninnah fifty dollars, he gave Hannah one hundred dollars. If he took Peninnah to Kings Island, he took Hannah to Cancun. There is a point where one could say, "I know it's bad that you can't have children, but wake up baby."

There is another point where one could argue that rather than be *content* Hannah should *contend*. She should fight and not settle for less than God's best.

Are you living with the tension of contentment versus contending? On the one hand you should be happy that you're married and have children; on the other hand you're more than a baby-making machine or a convenient sexual outlet. You have a brain, dreams, and visions. Sometimes you want to have a career, but you don't know if you can have a career and still be a good wife and mother. On the one hand you should be content, but there is something inside that makes you restless and unwilling to settle for less than God's best.

Men never have that problem. I never have to worry about leaving town, doing revivals, conferences, catching planes, whatever. I don't feel like anyone would say, "He's a bad husband. He's a bad father." They will say, "He's a successful man." But if my wife were hopping on and off planes, people would start saying negative things about her because there is always tension between contentment and contending.

Elkanah wanted to know why Hannah couldn't be happy with what she had. He took good care of her and couldn't understand why she wanted or needed more. Why was she complaining and crying? He didn't understand that while Hannah appreciated what he gave her, she had dreams and desires that a man could not fulfill.

That may be what some people are saying to you. "Why can't you be happy with what you have?" which is code language for, "Why don't you just settle?" But you know you can't, and you know why you can't, because there is too much inside of you.

Sisters must have wisdom and discernment to know whether to be content or to contend. Do you rest in being a single woman with a degree, career, house, and nice car, or do you fast and pray for a mate? Contend or content? What shall the sister be? You're an educated woman who has achieved success in life and people wonder why you're not satisfied with what you have. At night you wish for somebody to share with and talk to; you want to turn over and grab more than sheets and pillows. Are you being greedy for wanting more? Are you being ungrateful for what you already have? Wasn't that Hannah's dilemma?

Every woman has had a Hannah moment where she ponders, "Am I called to be content or to contend? Should I be content with what I have or go after the 'more' God has for me?" When you have an "I will not be denied" attitude, you will be misunderstood. A man can have that attitude and the world says that he is aggressive and strong. If a woman has that same attitude, she is bossy and pushy.

When you look at Hannah's story, you see why some people never rise up, move on, or go higher.

SOME WOMEN BECOME VICTIMS OF THEIR PROBLEMS

Hannah was barren. That was a problem because the value of a woman at that time was in her ability to give her husband a male child, an heir to his inheritance.

All of us have problems, but the key is to not let our problems confine or define us because they are temporary. Hannah got so caught up in her problems she couldn't see anything else. She was crying all the time, wasn't eating, emotional, moody, temperamental; her nerves were on edge and her skin was breaking out. She was having problems and it was because she allowed her problems to confine and define who she was.

You're more than your problems. Matter of fact, you're bigger and stronger than your problems.

SOME WOMEN ARE LIMITED
BY THEIR PERCEPTIONS

Because she was barren, Hannah saw herself as incomplete or less than a woman. She could not even fully receive the love of her husband because of her own issues. Elkanah had serious love for Hannah, but because she didn't feel complete, all that he did for her was misconstrued.

Let me say one word on behalf of the brothers. A lot of times you have frustrated husbands because they're doing all they know to do and you can't receive it. Sisters, sometimes the problem is not with him or them. I know you want to always make it him or them—your husband, the people on your job, the Church, or anyone that you feel is the cause of your major malfunction—but every now and then the problem is you. You may have to change your perception. However you see yourself is how you believe you deserve to be treated. Women who stay in violent relationships and allow themselves to be beaten up do so because somewhere in their psyche they are convinced they deserve to be beaten.

Your perception determines your reception. How you're perceived determines how you're received! For instance there are some people who don't care for me — don't feel bad about it; it's their loss — because I refuse to grovel, shuffle, or act like I'm unimportant. There was a time I would have done that, but not now. Consequently, when I go places it's amazing how people treat me based on how I perceive myself. When you walk like you belong and act like you belong, people will let you in even when you haven't been invited.

Listen to me sisters, *when you act like you are the cat's meow, somebody will meow your way!*

Some of what you're getting, you're asking for even if you don't know you're asking for it. Because you see yourself a certain way you send out subliminal messages: "I'm nothing, so you can overlook me." "You don't have to promote me; I'll train everybody who comes in here." "I'm not going to say anything because I'm just glad to be here." No! I'm releasing you today. There is some stuff you don't have to take anymore.

SOME WOMEN ARE VICTIMS
OF OTHER PEOPLE

Elkanah had a second wife named Peninnah who was a baby-making machine. She had sons and daughters and yet constantly provoked Hannah because she was jealous of her. Elkanah loved Hannah, and while Peninnah had given him numerous children, she didn't have his heart. While Hannah was crying, not eating, and having fits, the woman who was causing her grief wanted to take her place.

I'm trying to tell you that the woman you're worried about or jealous of is just as obsessed with you because she wants what you have. Peninnah envied Hannah because she had the love of Elkanah. If we're not careful, we will allow people to make us their hostage and rob us of our destiny. Thank God that in spite of all the things that were against her, Hannah rose up and her getting up shows you how to get up, too.

Chapter Three
It's Time to Get Busy

Have you ever talked with someone and realized the light was on but no one was home? You're steadily pouring out your heart and then you realize they're just not getting it. Elkanah wondered why Hannah wasn't happy with all the material things he had given her, plus his love. When Hannah realized her husband didn't understand, she went to the only One who could:

> . . . Whenever Hannah went up to the house of the Lord, her rival provoked her till she wept and would not eat. Elkanah her husband would say to her, "Hannah, why are you weeping? Why don't you eat? Why are you downhearted? Don't I mean more to you than ten sons?" Once when they had finished eating and drinking in Shiloh, **Hannah**

stood up. (1 Samuel 1:7-9(a), NIV, emphasis mine)

There comes a point in your life when your girlfriends, your mother, your sisters, and your cousins can't help you. You have to go to God in prayer with your petitions, pleas, and promises. He is the only one who really understands where you are and what you're going through:

> *In bitterness of soul Hannah wept much and prayed to the Lord. And she made a vow, saying, "O Lord Almighty, if you will only look upon your servant's misery and remember me, and not forget your servant but give her a son, then I will give him to the Lord for all the days of his life, and no razor will ever be used on his head."* (1 Samuel 1:10-11, NIV)

Every woman of God has resurrection power to get up. The song *Still I Rise* recorded by Yolanda Adams and composed by Percy Bady makes my point:

> Shattered, but I'm not broken. Wounded still time will heal. Heavy the load, the cross I bear. Lonely, the road I trod I

dare. Shaken, but here I stand. Weary, still I press on. Long are the nights, the tears I cry. Dark are the days, no sun in the skies.

Sometimes I'm troubled. But not is despair. Struggling, I make my way through. Trials they come to make me strong. I must endure, I must hold on. Above all my problems. Above all my eyes can see. Knowing God is able. To strengthen me.

Yet still I rise. Never to give up. Never to give in. Against all odds. Yet still I rise. High above the clouds. At times I feel low. Yet still I rise.

HANNAH ROSE WHILE STILL IN HER PAIN

When Hannah rose, her problem was not solved; yet, she still got up. Sometimes you try to wait for a perfect situation before you will act, move, or do something. There are no perfect situations. Sometimes you have to move in your pain, because staying is more painful. Can you testify to that?

<u>Pain is an indicator of the presence of life</u>. I could take you to the morgue and allow you to punch, kick, bite, or shoot a dead person and they wouldn't feel pain because there is no life. The fact that you feel pain means there is still life in you. If you didn't hurt, you wouldn't be alive. If what that person did to you didn't hurt you, it means you have killed a part of you. If your sin didn't hurt you, it means you have killed your conscience. If being betrayed by a friend didn't hurt you, it means you have killed your emotions. If the pain of the divorce didn't hurt you, it means you have killed your heart. The fact that you feel pain is an indicator of the presence of life. You hurt, but you're still alive.

<u>Pain is a sign that there is a problem</u>. Medical personnel will tell you that pain in the chest and shooting down your arm is an indicator of a heart attack. It is not a heart attack, just a sign that you have a problem. God allows pain in your life as a sign that you have a problem. You have been trying to ignore it and make it go away and you can't. It's like saying

there is nothing wrong with your husband hitting you because he only does it when he is drunk! You have a problem and God allows the presence of pain to point that out.

Pain is a way to healing. Sometimes the way the doctor knows that you're healing is when you begin to feel pain. You know you're getting better because you can hurt. Have you ever intentionally and deliberately shut down so that you would not hurt anymore? I did it at a teenager. I made a decision to shut down because I figured it was a sure way to not ever be hurt again. It wasn't until I let myself feel pain that I knew I was getting better. Sometimes you have to hurt in order to feel better.

HANNAH ROSE AND RECEIVED A PROMISE THAT RESULTED IN PERFORMANCE

Eli was the priest on duty when Hannah was in the temple praying. Because he only saw her lips moving and didn't hear any words, he assumed she was drunk. When he confronted her, Hannah assured him that she hadn't had anything to drink; she was pouring her heart out to the Lord. Eli believed her:

67

Eli answered, "Go in peace, and may the God of Israel grant you what you have asked of him." She said, "May your servant find favor in your eyes." Then she went her way and ate something, and her face was no longer downcast. (1 Samuel 1:17-18, NIV)

The next day Hannah rose up early and worshiped before the Lord, and that is what you need to do. If you will start worshiping, you will stop crying. If you will start worshiping, you will stop being sad, being depressed, staying awake at night pacing the floor, feeling sorry for yourself. Hannah got up early, worshiped God, and returned home and got busy:

Early the next morning they arose and worshiped before the Lord and then went back to their home at Ramah. Elkanah lay with Hannah his wife, and the Lord remembered her. So in the course of time Hannah conceived and gave birth to a son. She named him Samuel, saying, "Because I asked the Lord for him." (1 Samuel 1:19, NIV)

I like my paraphrase of 1 Samuel 1:19 better: Hannah shouted, thanked God, cut a step, spoke in tongues, went home, put on a negligee and said, "There's a time to speak in tongues and a time to get busy. I've spoken, now let's get busy!"

Take those Bibles out of your bed so your husband can find you. Stop wearing his undershirt and take those curlers out of your hair. There is a time to shout and there is a time to get busy.

For those of you who aren't married, get busy going back to school, writing a business plan, and making something out of your life. It is not just about getting busy between the sheets. Stop sitting around the house looking at the four walls. Get up and do something with your life. Get busy on a plan for what you have to do. Begin making preparations for what God is going to do in your life.

Chapter Four
God Is Changing Your Name

---

*Y*our new name is Hannah Rose. It is a beautiful name. If my wife and I had another baby, I would name her Hannah Rose.

You are Hannah Rose. No matter what you face or what you go through, if the Lord is with you then remember:

> *Ye are of God, little children, and have over-come them: because greater is he that is in you, than he that is in the world.* (1 John 4:4, KJV)

If God is for you, He is more than the world against you. You can rise. In your pain and with your problems, you can get up. God is calling you to get up and walk into your destiny, your future, and your purpose. God is calling you to be a 21st Century Hannah Rose.

Has anyone ever done this before? Look around you. Look over your shoulder. You have known and are surrounded by fellow sisters in the spirit, other women named Hannah Rose who overcame setbacks, trials, and difficulties. They made it and now cheer you on. They are telling you that you can make it, too. You can rise above your circumstances. Whatever you have been through, whatever you have faced, whatever you have had to deal with in the past may have stung, shocked, startled, surprised, and even saddened you. But you know what? It didn't stop you. You made it. You survived it. You faced it, overcame it, and now you are stronger because of it. May I be so bold as to suggest how you now handle and process whatever you went through?

- You savor it. Don't rush or run from it. Take a moment to reflect on it. Why? Because it was a defining moment in your life and it helped make you who you are.

72

- You share it. Don't waste your experience. It wasn't just about you. Some other sista girl needs to know and hear your story. Don't be afraid or ashamed to tell others what God has done for you.

- You shout about it. Go ahead and cut your step. Give God a holler. You have a right to praise Him! What the devil meant for your destruction has turned out for your good.

Now that you have made it, you owe God some praise. In fact, wait a minute and let me start with you:

Father in the name of Jesus, I bless you for every woman who reads this book. God, I thank you for the honor of depositing into their lives. I have given them what you whispered to me. You told me to tell your women that Hannah rose, and it was time for them to get up, too. God, I have done what you told me to do. I have finished my assignment.

I pray for every woman reading this book and I am asking in the name of Jesus for your spirit, anointing, and power to fall fresh on them. May they rise and go to new heights, levels, and dimensions. God, make them a modern day Hannah.

Many wrestled with the revelation and illumination of how to handle the tension between contentment and contending. I pray you will give them discernment and wisdom to be wives and mothers and still be women of destiny, excellence, and purpose.

To those who are still believing you for a mate or waiting for the unfolding of your purpose, your plan, and will, help them to trust you, walk with you, and know that you are leading and guiding them.

Lord, I pray that you will fulfill every Word spoken in their lives; everything you have planned for them before they were conceived and born. I impart to them the blessings of the Lord, the favor of God. I impart to them your perfect plan for their lives. Every good thing you have purposed for them to have, I impart to them now.

I thank you that it is done and it shall be. In Jesus' name. Amen.

Help for Those Who Hurt

This book is dedicated to my wife and children for their unwavering love, support, and encouragement.

Table of Contents

You may not know me, but I know you. I may not know your name, your address or even the particulars of your life, but I know you.

I know you. You are a hard-working, law-abiding, God-honoring man who, in spite of what the television portrays and the media tries to insinuate, is really doing the best you can to lead your family, serve your community and make a contribution to the world in which you live.

I know you. You are a mother, a woman, who just wants to do right. You work, cook, and clean; yet, you know there is more to life than pots, pans, and dirty clothes. You want to know your purpose and you want to realize your destiny. You have heard it all, seen it all, and you are not impressed. You want more, but deep down inside you are not sure you can or should have more.

I know you. You are a child, a teenager, or a young adult, living in a world so different from any other generation. Violence, disease, uncertainty, and confusion all mark the world you live in; a world without moral absolutes. Somewhere, someone has taken down the road signs and left you to navigate life on your own.

I know you. You are a senior citizen, living in an age and world that glamorizes youth and beauty. You used to have meaning in life; you used to look forward to each new day, one filled with new challenges. Now you sit alone with no one to talk to and seemingly no reason to live. Questions like, "Who am I?" "Where do I fit in?" "Why am I still here?" fill your days and nights and, yet, no answers come.

I know you. You just left the grave of the one you love and your last memories of them are tubes, buttons, machines, or regret for words never said, apologies never made, or love never affirmed. All that is left are memories, a fresh mound of dirt, and the aching question of why?

I know you. You just opened an envelope and found a pink slip, or received a diagnosis of a devastating illness, or perhaps you have just left divorce court.

I know you. You are the person who puts on a happy face, keeps a stiff upper lip, and pretends that everything is okay, but inside you hurt.

So how do I know you? I am a fellow sufferer. I know hurt, pain, failure, and regret. What I want to share with you is the hope available for those who hurt. The answers don't and won't come easy. The solutions will not arrive overnight. The pain is not easily erased. Yet, there is hope. There is help. There is healing.

Here is the good news: Life is not futile, failure is not fatal, and death is not final. As a matter of fact, the really good news is that you can sing again and dance once more. It might be with a limp or through tears, but the music has started and they are playing our song. It is the symphony of the broken, the melody of the hurting, and a song for people on their way back.

How Did I Ever Get Here?

---

*S*everal years ago I read a book by Dr. Lloyd Ogilvie in which he wrote about the need and importance of knowing what time it is in our lives. Dr. Ogilvie didn't mean chronological time such as years, age, or time as it relates to numbers; he was speaking of seasons, timing, destiny, and purpose of our lives.

I am convinced that one of the things that traps us and stops us from reaching our destiny is that we are ignorant of our times and season. As a result of us not knowing the time, we also don't know our place.

So let me ask you a question: Where are you right now? I don't mean physically, but where are you in your life? More importantly, are you where you dreamed, hoped, and planned to be at this season of your life?

In order to truthfully answer that question, you need to go back into your past and remember, or maybe rediscover, what it was you used to dream about, talk about, and think about.

Do you remember your childhood, the games you used to play, the roles you took on, and the dreams you used to have? What was it you dreamed about doing and being? When did your mind and spirit soar? When did your imagination take flight?

Please don't dismiss these questions as insignificant. Those first dreams, thoughts, and visions may well be an indication of what you were really meant to do. Perhaps where you are now is because of how far you have strayed from where you were meant to be. Here is what I believe with all of my heart: Every person is born for a specific reason and a specific purpose. The great tragedy is that few of us know or believe that, and even fewer of us ever realize our potential.

Some years ago, I challenged First Church to ask God this question, "What was on your mind the moment you made me?" I am convinced that the answer to that question contains the key to unlocking the riddle to our lives. Yet, it is a question many are uncomfortable with because it presupposes:

- That God knows me, intimately and personally.

- That God thinks about me and I am on His mind.

- That I have an assignment to fulfill here on earth; thus, I am accountable and responsible for that assignment and purpose.

Many people are uncomfortable with this theory because they are not accustomed to thinking of themselves as being important and significant enough to matter to God. But we are:

> *The LORD gave me this message: "I knew you before I formed you in your mother's womb. Before you were born I set you apart and appointed you as my prophet to the nations." "O Sovereign LORD," I said, "I can't speak for you! I'm too young!" The LORD replied, "Don't say, 'I'm too young,' for you must go wherever I send you and say whatever I tell you" . . . "For I know the plans I have for you," says the LORD. "They are plans for good and not for disaster, to give*

you a future and a hope." (Jeremiah 1:4-7, 29:11, NLT)

I praise you because I am fearfully and wonderfully made; your works are wonderful, I know that full well. (Psalm 139:14, NIV)

Let me tell you what I know about you: You were made for a purpose and I believe that one day you will discover that purpose. This is so important because I believe the reason some of us find ourselves in places wondering, "How did I ever get here?" is because of our failing to understand our value, purpose, and destiny.

You are trapped in an abusive relationship because you don't believe you deserve more. You have convinced yourself that you are ugly, unwanted, overweight, and undesirable and so you settle. But in your heart you wonder, "How did I ever get here?"

You are trapped in a dead-end job—not because you can't handle responsibility—but because you have been told (and now you believe it) that you are dumb, stupid, limited, and not deserving.

You may feel that way and at times have wondered, "How did I ever get here?"

You are trapped in a pit of anger, unforgiveness, and bitterness with no laughter, no joy, and no music. You tell yourself that the hurt will never go away, the pain can never be relieved, and the memories can never be erased. You want to smile, to laugh, and to even love again, but you're so afraid and alone. You have wondered, and even prayed, "Lord, how did I ever get here?"

You wonder is there any way out of this? And the answer is yes!

One of my favorite scenes from the movie *Gandhi* takes place when the Mahatmas, portrayed by Ben Kingsley, is confronted by a male visitor. Gandhi is on a self-imposed fast until the violence between the Hindu and Moslem Indians ceases. The man throws a piece of bread at Gandhi and says, "Here, eat; I don't want your blood on my hands. I am going to hell." Gandhi, from his mat of misery, replies in a weakened voice, "I know a way out of hell." My friend, where you are now and what you're going through may seem like hell, but there is a way out.

Chances are that where you are is not where you were meant to be, and it is certainly not where you were meant to stay. God has a plan for your life, a purpose for your experience, and a testing that He wants to take you through. Let me suggest three things that I believe will help you get past where you are and put you on the road to where God wants to take you:

- Assess where you are. This begins with a simple question, Where am I? This question can be answered in several ways: Where am I emotionally, relationally, chronologically and spiritually. What is going on in my life right now? Do an honest appraisal. Don't be too easy or too hard on yourself. Sit down, take inventory, and gauge where you are. Jesus talks about doing this when He teaches about counting the cost and suggests that you should sit down and see if you have adequate resources to finish what you have started. Keep in mind that assessing ourselves or our condition doesn't mean we do nothing about them. It means we count the costs and we develop a plan and strategy to get us from where we are to where God wants us to be.

- Accept where you are. This does not mean giving into where we are. We honestly look at where we are and say these are the facts, but now what is the truth? What is the difference you ask? Simply, but powerfully, the difference is this: The facts are what exist or what is; the truth is what can be. It is really what God says. The Bible calls it faith and it is how we are to live.

- Affirm that where you are is not your ultimate destiny. What do you believe about yourself? *"For I can do everything through Christ, who gives me strength"* (Philippians 4:13, NLT). Is this what you believe? If it is, then you know what lies ahead. You know that what God has in store for you is infinitely better than what you have or where you are now. Bishop Charles E. Blake puts it this way: "I see you in your future and you look better than you do right now."

The three previous steps are crucial and key for dealing with where we are. However, I must also show you some steps that will get you beyond where you are. Let me caution you that these next steps are more personal and difficult, but not impossible, to achieve:

- Recognize where you are. The reason this is painful at times is because it may mean that we have to own up to or admit our culpability in our situation. It may also mean that we have to honestly identify persons in our lives who have played a role in our being where we are. There are only two types of people in your life: Givers and takers or helpers and hurters. You must know who is around you.

- Release. This may involve forgiving and releasing both yourself and others. In my opinion there is no greater bondage than that which is held against us for sins and mistakes of the past. One of the most effective tools the devil uses is the tool of guilt for the mess and mistakes on our part, and unforgiveness for hurts and wrongs inflicted by others. We must learn how to walk in the freedom Christ has given us. One component of that freedom is justification. Someone has said that means God sees us "just as if I" had never sinned. Not only must we forgive ourselves, but we must also forgive others. When we hold people and refuse to forgive, we not only stay in bondage to the memory and power of what happened, but we also cancel forgiveness for ourselves. The power of release is real and awesome.

- Remove. There are times you have to leave where you are, your surroundings and even your friends. This is what God told Abram, *"The LORD had said to Abram, "Go from your country, your people and your father's household to the land I will show you"* (Genesis 12:1, NIV). Abram would never have received God's promise or God's best by staying where he was. In order to get more, Abram had to remove himself and step out on the road to something new. At times you and I must do the same thing. Someone has said that insanity is doing the same thing and expecting different results. In order to get something new, you have to do something new.

Perhaps you feel that where you are is beyond your control. An illness, a job termination, or an accident that has left you disabled has taken things out of your hands. Your pain is real. Allow me to share something I discovered during a difficult and fearful time in my life when I was battling a devastating illness. One of my members, Mary Goode (who has since gone on to glory), sent me a card with an article enclosed entitled *Don't Waste Your Suffering*. That is the word I want to share with you. Whatever you are experiencing and going through, don't waste it. If God has permitted it or allowed it, He has purposed good to come out of it: *"And we know that all things work together for good to them that love God, to them who are the called according to his purpose"* (Romans 8:28, KJV). So what then should be our response?

<u>Don't become bitter</u>. I know from personal experience that there is a natural tendency to get angry, lash out, or curse our fate when something negative happens. While it is normal to feel anxious, uncer-

tain, or even afraid, we must guard against bitterness. Bitterness exhibits itself in hostility, unforgiveness, and a critical and even ungrateful attitude.

Several years ago I had the opportunity to host an interfaith gathering and one of the speakers was the late Dr. Martin Luther King, Sr. Once the crowd had gone home, a few of us had an opportunity to share with Daddy King in a small private setting. Someone asked him how he handled his losses without becoming bitter and he answered, as only a man of his maturity and wisdom could, "I don't dwell on what I've lost. I just thank God for what I have left." This response came from someone who could have been filled with hatred, bitterness, and resentment, but he chose to focus and dwell on the positive aspects of life; by doing so he became a healer and a leader instead of a whiner and loser.

Like Daddy King you may have had losses in your life, but don't you have something left? I am sure the answer is yes, so why not begin to thank God for that. Doing so has the power to change your life.

<u>Guard against depression</u>. This is not always easy, especially when certain medications are involved.

95

Sickness sometimes produces depression. I discovered during my recuperation that daily reading of the Word, prayer, and a heart of gratitude helped me to avoid depression. And when I couldn't ward it off, these things helped me to deal with it.

<u>Never give up</u>. Most of us have heard the story of Great Britain's Prime Minister, Winston Churchill, who had been invited to give the commencement address at the Harrow School in England. Mr. Churchill stood up, fixed his gaze on the class before him, and said, "Never give up. Never give up. Never. Never. Never give up." He then sat down.

These are my words to you. I can only imagine your pain, your questions, and your fears; yet, I hear the psalmist say, *"What time I am afraid, I will trust in thee"* (Psalm 56:3, KJV). My friend, don't give up. Don't surrender. God loves you. He has not abandoned you and He still has a plan for your life.

Life Is Not Futile

One of my heroes is the late Dr. Martin Luther King, Jr., and one of my favorite books is his *Strength to Love*, which is a compilation of his sermons. The book contains several poems and quotes that I have committed to memory. The first is a poem by Paul Laurence Dunbar entitled *Life*, which says in part:

> A crust of bread and a corner to sleep in.
> A minute to smile and an hour to weep in.
> A pint of joy to a peck of trouble.
> And never a laugh, but moans come double.
> And that is life!

The other quote comes from William Shakespeare: "Life is a tale, told by an idiot, full of sound and fury, signifying nothing." For many, these verses sum up not only what they think about life, but also what they have experienced in life, which is a greater tragedy and reality. Yet, when we read the Bible, that is not at all God's plan or will for us. Someone has said that the great pursuit of life is to ask the question, "What is the meaning of life?" I want to suggest that perhaps the more vital question might be, "What is my purpose in life?" You and I are here for a reason; the pursuit of our lives ought to be to find out what that reason is.

God has a plan for every person in this world and we should give ourselves over to discovering the plan. Do you know why most people never come to that place in their lives? It is because of one simple thing: They believe the lie that Satan tells them about life and themselves. If you have fallen into that trap, don't feel bad. You are neither the first person this has happened to nor the first generation that has fallen victim and succumbed to this lie. This problem is as old as time.

Several years ago there was a popular song among the religious community with a line that raised the question: "Whose report will you believe?" Unfortunately, many people prefer to believe the report of the enemy and, thus, miss out on God's best for their lives. This is exactly what Satan did to Adam and Eve. He sold them a bill of goods and convinced them that the lie he told on God was actually truth.

In love and mercy, God created a perfect world and then created two perfect people. God not only put them in the Garden of Eden, but He gave them dominion and authority over all of creation. There was only one stipulation: Don't eat of the tree in the middle of the garden. The devil came along and suggested that this prohibition by God could only mean one thing: God was trying to keep something good from them. The devil influenced Adam and Eve to rebel against God.

I never read the Genesis account without getting angry at Adam and Eve. They were in a perfect environment with power and authority over all they saw. They were not only in communion with God, but they were also made in the image of God; yet, they threw it all away in an attempt to get what they already had.

This account reminds me of a story about a dog walking past a lake with a bone in his mouth. Looking into the water, the dog saw what he thought was another dog with a bone. Seeking to get that bone, the dog opened his mouth to bark at the dog in the lake. When he opened his mouth to bark, the bone that was in his mouth fell into the lake. The moral of this story is that you can lose what you have trying to get something else. That is what Adam and Eve did. They forfeited their unique connection to and their relationship with God on the word of an imposter and an interloper. The tragedy is that there are people today who listen to Satan's lies and miss out on the best that God has for them.

You may be wondering how you can know that God has a plan for your life. Read the creation story in the Book of Genesis. It tells you what God had on His mind when He created the first people and placed them in this world:

> *So God created human beings in his own image. In the image of God he created them; male and female he created them. Then God blessed them and said, "Be fruitful and multiply. Fill the earth and govern it. Reign over the fish in the sea, the birds in the sky, and all the animals that scurry along the ground." Then God said, "Look! I have given you every seed-bearing plant throughout the earth and all the fruit trees for your food. And I have given every green plant as food for all the wild animals, the birds in the sky, and the*

small animals that scurry along the ground – everything that has life." And that is what happened. Then God looked over all he had made, and he saw that it was very good! And evening passed and morning came, marking the sixth day. (Genesis 1:27-31, NLT)

Do you notice what God had in mind for His creation? It was a life of fellowship with Him. It was a life of mastery and productivity. It was a life of union and true intimacy. It was a life of total health and true prosperity. Does that sound like a life of depravation, denial, or lack? Not to me. In fact, it sounds like the life I want.

If we're honest, we will admit that people seldom really live that way. Why is that? I believe it is because we have chosen to accept what Satan has told us about God and life. As a result of accepting the lie, we have forfeited our opportunity to walk in and experience the kind of life God intended us to have. Yet, we just saw in the above verses the way God wills and desires for us to live.

I must admit that much of what I have shared up to now may not have been very positive or encouraging, but I have good news for you. Life is not futile. There is meaning and purpose to our days and our lives. As a matter of fact, God wants to add life to your days and meaning to your life. That is His will, desire, and plan. Let me give you one verse of Scripture that says it better than I ever could. Jesus says, *"I am come that they might have life, and that they might have it more abundantly"* (John 10:10, KJV).

That verse should make you smile, shout, run, or do something. In fact, it gets better, because in the verse before this Jesus says: *"The thief cometh not, but for to steal, and to kill, and to destroy. . ."* (John 10:9, KJV). I will give you one guess as to who the thief is, and if you guessed Satan, you are correct. Jesus says that Satan has been lying on the Father and deceiving His children, but Jesus takes the time to set the record straight: I am here so that you can have life. And not just life, but life in abundance, an overflowing life (life with some to spare). Now that is the truth, the whole truth, and nothing but the truth!

You may be asking: If all of that is true, why are so many people not living that way? Why it is that saved people who claim to have the Lord in their lives don't seem to show, exhibit, or experience the kind of life that the Bible talks about? How is that? Well, the answer is simple. You can go to church, read the Bible, and even say your prayers, but if you don't truly believe what you say or pray it does you no good.

Suppose you accept a dinner invitation and on the day of the dinner you take special care with how you dress, you show up on time, and even bring a gift for the host or hostess. The table is spread with an assortment of delicious food, but you don't eat. The food is there, you are there, and you have been invited to dine, but you don't eat. The end result is that the food, although good, nutritious, and available, does you no good if you don't partake of it. The same holds true about life and spiritual things. The promises of God are true, real, and available. His plan for your life is good, but you have to do more than just show up. You have to believe and that requires faith and action.

Your life is not a joke or the result of a cruel game played on you by God. Your life has meaning and purpose. God has a plan for your life that is bigger and better than anything you could ever dream up for yourself. It is your destiny, your purpose, and your reason for being alive.

Can you imagine what it would be like to live your purpose? To do more than just hold down a job, punch a clock, or drag through the day? Can you imagine what it would be like to be fully alive, full of life, to know why you were born and then be doing that? That is what God wants you to have. That is how He wants you to live.

You have to believe it and then step out in faith just like Peter did when he walked on water:

> *Shortly before dawn Jesus went out to them, walking on the lake. When the disciples saw him walking on the lake, they were terrified. "It's a ghost," they said, and cried out in fear. But Jesus immediately said to them: "Take courage! It is I. Don't be afraid." "Lord, if it's you," Peter replied, "tell me to come to you on the water." "Come," he said. Then Peter got down out of the boat, walked on the water and came toward Jesus. But when he saw the wind, he was afraid and, beginning to sink, cried out, "Lord, save me!" Immediately Jesus reached out his hand and caught him. "You of little faith," he said, "why did you doubt?"* (Matthew 14:25-31, NIV)

You and I must learn from Peter's example and never take our eyes off of Jesus as we walk toward Him.

Failure Is Not Fatal

$\mathcal{C}$an I ask you a question: Have you ever failed at anything? Okay, now that you have picked yourself up off the floor and stopped laughing, of course the answer is yes. If you're like me, the answer would more likely be, "How many times today?" All of us are well acquainted with failure, and although we may laugh now, we know that failure is painful and that the sting of it hurts like few other things in our lives. When you compound that reality with public failure, sometimes the pain and shame of it is almost too great to bear.

I have some encouraging news for you: Failure is not fatal. That's right; failure does not disqualify you from the game of life. Neither does it mean you can never be used of God. If that were so, the Bible would be very thin because everyone God used experienced failure at some point and place in their life. If you have failed; if it seems like your life is a series of failures or if you are trying to make a comeback and rebound from failure, you need to know that you are in good company. Your failure, no matter how recent, how public, how painful, or how bad, is not fatal. There is life after failure.

I know you have read the Bible, but have you *really* read the Bible? I have and what amazes me is how many times we are allowed to see the failures of the men and women God used. I have often said that one of the greatest arguments for the divine inspiration of the Scripture is that the Bible is so honest and transparent. It puts people's business out there with stuff I am sure that the subjects of the stories would just as well have been left out.

Adam and Eve sinned. Abel murdered his brother, Cain. Moses had a temper. Noah got drunk. Samson had a weakness. David allowed lust to overcome his common sense. Solomon lacked discipline. And on and on, and that is just a partial list from the Old Testament! I am not endorsing misbehavior, but I am pointing out that God has experience in dealing with and redeeming people who have experienced failure.

I believe one of the most powerful stories about failure and restoration is found in the New Testament and centers on a man named Peter, one of the disciples of Jesus. While most of us are familiar with the events that took place on the night that Jesus was arrested, the story begins before that and teaches us something about how God deals with our failures.

Jesus had already told Peter that Satan was out to get him; yet, listen to what Jesus says:

> *But I have prayed for you, Simon, that your faith may not fail. And when you have turned back, strengthen your brothers.* (Luke 22:32, NIV)

Peter denied that anything would happen, but Jesus knew what was ahead:

> *But he replied, "Lord, I am ready to go with you to prison and to death." Jesus answered, "I tell you, Peter, before the rooster crows today, you will deny three times that you know me."* (Luke 22:33-34, NIV)

Now fast forward to after the crucifixion. Jesus has risen from the dead and the angel gives Mary these instructions:

> *But go, tell his disciples and Peter, 'He is*
> *going ahead of you into Galilee. There you*
> *will see him, just as he told you.' (Mark 16:7,*
> *NIV)*

You should be shouting right now! Jesus is request-
ing an audience with Peter who just a few days prior
had sworn with an oath, "I don't know the man!"
But wait, there's more:

> *Afterward Jesus appeared again to his dis-*
> *ciples, by the Sea of Galilee. It happened this*
> *way: Simon Peter, Thomas (also known as*
> *Didymus), Nathanael from Cana in Galilee,*
> *the sons of Zebedee, and two other disciples*
> *were together. "I'm going out to fish," Simon*
> *Peter told them, and they said, "We'll go*
> *with you." So they went out and got into the*
> *boat, but that night they caught nothing.*
> *Early in the morning, Jesus stood on the*
> *shore, but the disciples did not realize that it*
> *was Jesus. He called out to them, "Friends,*
> *haven't you any fish?" "No," they answered.*
> *He said, "Throw your net on the right side of*
> *the boat and you will find some." When they*
> *did, they were unable to haul the net in be-*

cause of the large number of fish. Then the disciple whom Jesus loved said to Peter, "It is the Lord!" As soon as Simon Peter heard him say, "It is the Lord," he wrapped his outer garment around him (for he had taken it off) and jumped into the water. The other disciples followed in the boat, towing the net full of fish, for they were not far from shore, about a hundred yards. When they landed, they saw a fire of burning coals there with fish on it, and some bread. Jesus said to them, "Bring some of the fish you have just caught." So Simon Peter climbed back into the boat and dragged the net ashore. It was full of large fish, 153, but even with so many the net was not torn. Jesus said to them, "Come and have breakfast." None of the disciples dared ask him, "Who are you?" They knew it was the Lord. Jesus came, took the bread and gave it to them, and did the same with the fish. This was now the third time Jesus appeared to his disciples after he was raised from the dead. When they had finished eating, Jesus said to Simon Peter, "Simon son of John, do you love me more than these?" (John 21:1-19, NIV)

Sitting around a fire with his disciples, Jesus turns to Peter: *"Simon, do you love me?"* Wait a minute! Why didn't Jesus ask, "Peter, how could you do this to me? Or, "Man, what were you thinking?" Or "As far as I'm concerned, you're dead. You don't exist!" Jesus could have said all of that and more, but He didn't. He simply asked, *"Do you love me?"* A friend of mine, Pastor Jim Cook, helped me to see something about this passage: This encounter takes place around a fire and Peter's denial took place around a fire. God brought Peter full circle to a place of full repentance.

You might not believe this, but there is still more to this story. When the Church was launched on the day of Pentecost (Acts 2:14-41), guess who the keynote speaker was? Peter. God had brought him from failure to fruitfulness. And the good news is that He wants to do the same for you.

You may not have done what Peter did, but you have your own story of failure. Perhaps you have spent time in jail. Perhaps you have had a moral failure in your life. Perhaps you dropped out of school. Perhaps you have just gotten a divorce or lost your job or are pregnant out of wedlock. It could be any of these or a hundred other failures. Here is what I want and need you to believe: Whatever the failure, it is not fatal. You can come back from it. How do I know? I'm glad you asked.

- Mercy. Everything starts with the mercy of God. Mercy is more than pity and more than even compassion. Mercy is kindness to those who don't deserve it. Jesus could have rejected Peter, blackballed, and humiliated him, but instead He showed mercy and treated him with kindness. The mercy of God is still available to you, even in your failure. In fact, it is available *because* of your failure since you would not need it otherwise. How do you get mercy? You come clean with God and ask for it without excuses. Just say, "I failed, Lord. Please have mercy."

- Grace. Do you have any idea how differently the story could have been or what would have happened if Peter had gotten what he deserved? What saved Peter? Grace, the unmerited favor of God. Someone has said that grace is *not* getting what we deserve. Peter did not deserve a second chance, but he was given one. You and I don't deserve another chance at life, love, ministry, family, or career, but in grace God gives it to us. No wonder Isaac Watts could write about *Amazing Grace*. For those of us who have experienced it, grace truly and gloriously is amazing.

- Forgiveness. Did you notice that at no time in the story does Jesus say to Peter, "I forgive you?" I think that the reason for that is Jesus had already forgiven Peter, not on the cross when Jesus said, *"Father, forgive them,"* but on the day He told Peter, *"I have prayed for you."* You can't pray for someone you hate or someone you are holding something against. What does that mean? It means that Jesus saw what Peter was going to do and even before he did it, He forgave him. You and I are given that same forgiveness when we fail. We come to Jesus who already knows us, loves us, and is able to recycle our lives and uses us even stained and scarred. We become forgiven and act as living trophies of His grace, mercy, and love.

This chapter contains some of the best news I know: Our failures don't have the power to destroy or stop us. We can come back from failure. We can rise and soar. We can sing and dance because failure is not fatal.

Death Is Not Final

On the Sunday after September 11, 2001, I stood in the pulpit of First Church of God and sought to bring a word of hope from the Word of God. I do not know if what I said answered any questions or put to rest any of the deep seated fears that all of us felt that week, but I remember saying then—and time has borne me out—that our lives changed that day and that somehow we sensed that nothing, including us, would ever be the same. Someone used the phrase "the new normal" which lets us know that our lives had been changed forever.

What was September 11, 2001 really all about? I believe it was more than an assault on America; more than an attack on the World Trade Center, and even more than an ambush on our country. In essence, I believe it was an affront to our way of life and the real purpose was to strike terror in our hearts and cause us to lose our sense of security and confidence. Did the terrorist succeed?

The verdict is still out, but this much we know: Right after the attack Americans were afraid. The fear was brought on by watching people, just like us, being swept into eternity in a flash of time. The police commissioner was asked about his most vivid memory and he responded, "It was getting to Ground Zero minutes after the second plane crashed and watching people jump out of windows thousands of feet from the ground." On September 11, 2001 we saw death — not on a movie screen or in a hospital or senior citizens home — but we saw the death of people who weren't supposed to die and it reminded us of how frail we really are.

Few things are more sobering than coming face-to-face with our own mortality — *"Whereas ye know not what shall be on the morrow. For what is your life? It is even a vapour, that appeareth for a little time, and then vanisheth away"* (James 4:14, KJV) — and that indeed we can be here today and gone today, all in a moment of time. That is why the words of Moses have never been truer: *"Teach us to number our days, that we may gain a heart of wisdom"* (Psalm 90:12, NIV).

What is it that makes us fear death so much? All of our lives, and even throughout history, people have feared death. The writer of Hebrews says, "*...and free those who all their lives were held in slavery by their fear of death*" (Hebrews 2:15, NIV). Do you know what that means? It means that as long as we fear death, we cannot ever really live. It isn't until we conquer death that we experience life in its fullness. In other words, when we fear death, we die all the time. We never really live.

What is death? The dictionary defines it, "as a permanent cessation of all vital functions; the end of life." A theological answer would be, "the point of separation from this life to another." For those who are saved, it is the entrance into eternal life with God; for those who are lost or without God, it is the eternal separation from God.

Why do we fear death? I believe the answer is two-fold: First, because of the unknown. Despite the best efforts of Hollywood, authors, and even some preachers, no one knows what happens when you die. The Word of God tells us that our bodies go back to the dust and our spirits go back to God, but for specific details the Bible doesn't say much about the state of death. People who die are said to be at rest, asleep, or in the presence of God:

119

Jesus said, "There was a certain rich man who was splendidly clothed in purple and fine linen and who lived each day in luxury. At his gate lay a poor man named Lazarus who was covered with sores. As Lazarus lay there longing for scraps from the rich man's table, the dogs would come and lick his open sores. Finally, the poor man died and was carried by the angels to be with Abraham. The rich man also died and was buried, and his soul went to the place of the dead. There, in torment, he saw Abraham in the far distance with Lazarus at his side. The rich man shouted, 'Father Abraham, have some pity! Send Lazarus over here to dip the tip of his finger in water and cool my tongue. I am in anguish in these flames.' But Abraham said to him, 'Son, remember that during your lifetime you had everything you wanted, and Lazarus had nothing. So now he is here being comforted, and you are in anguish. And besides, there is a great chasm separating us. No one can cross over to you from here, and no one can cross over to us from there.' Then the rich man said, 'Please, Father Abraham, at least send him to my father's home. For I have five brothers, and I want him to warn them so they don't end up in this place of torment.' But Abraham said, 'Moses and the prophets have warned them. Your brothers can read what they wrote.' The rich man replied, 'No, Father Abraham! But if someone is sent to them from the dead, then they will repent of their sins and turn to God.' But Abraham said, 'If they won't listen to Moses and the prophets, they won't listen even if someone rises from the dead." (Luke 16:19-31, NLT)

We know from this parable that even in eternity we will have knowledge, feeling, and consciousness. We still know very little about what happens when we die and await the return of Jesus. The unknown is fearful and disconcerting.

The second reason we fear death is because of the finality of it. Anyone who has lost a loved one knows that the most difficult moment of that experience is when the casket is about to be closed for the final time. There is an ache that is produced by the knowledge that we will never see them again, at least not in this life. It all seems so final.

121

The Christian answer to this fear of death is that Christ has obtained the victory over death for us. When Christians gather on Sunday, especially Easter Sunday, we do so in celebration and faith in the resurrection of Christ from the grave. His triumph gives us hope even in the face of death.

There are three truths that our faith in Christ establishes for us that give us confidence as we face the vicissitudes of life:

- The pain of death has been removed. *"O death, where is thy sting? O grave, where is thy victory?"* (1 Corinthians 15:55, KJV). The answer, of course, is that Christ has taken the sting and pain of death and removed it. As believers we don't have to fear death because the pain of it has been dealt with by Jesus.

- The power of death has been broken. Since Adam, death has reigned as an unconquered champion, leveling everyone in its wake and path. Like a fighter with a perfect record, death was undefeated until Jesus. In that garden tomb, a battle was fought between Jesus and Satan, and in the end, Jesus emerged victorious: *"I am he that liveth, and was dead; and, behold, I am alive for evermore, Amen; and have the keys of hell and of death"* (Revelation 1:18, KJV).

- The penalty of death has been paid. In the garden, after the fall of Adam and Eve, the penalty for their disobedience was physical death, which was the ultimate price for their insurrection. It was a debt passed onto all of us. The good news is as the songwriter wrote, "Jesus paid it all!"

It is for these very reasons that believers can face life and death with calm assurance. We rest in what Christ has done for us.

There are those of you who may be suffering loss on another level. Your pain comes from the death of a marriage, a career, or a friendship. Your pain is real and your grief is genuine. You need to know that Jesus can bring life to what looks like dead situations. Even if He chooses not to resurrect the marriage, the job, or the friendship, He can and will heal you and help you face the future because He is with you. As I close this chapter, embrace the lyrics to *Because He Lives* by songwriter William Gaither:

> God sent His son. They called Him Jesus.
> He came to love, heal, and forgive.
> He lived and died to buy my pardon.
> An empty grave is there to prove my Savior lives.
> Because He lives, I can face tomorrow.
> Because He lives, all fear is gone.
> Because I know He holds the future,
> Life is worth the living just because He lives.

Epilogue

*W*ell, you made it! I know at times you may have doubted that you would or questioned whether the trip was worth it, but here you are at the end of this book and in some ways at the end of your search.

I know that for some of you it has been a difficult and painful journey. I am sure there have been things you might not have thought about for years, maybe even some things you have been trying to forget, but you faced them. Perhaps you discovered that just like the giant monster lurking under the bed of a child that these things were not as ferocious as you thought.

Having made the journey, let's now look at how we get back on track. Remember we started out asking, "How did I ever get here?" Now it is time to move on, but to where? I believe that all of our searching is really for God, and what we think we can find in things or people can really only be found in Him. For some of you this is a difficult statement because you feel that where you are right now is God's fault. Trusting Him may seem difficult, if not impossible. But please believe me, God is your only hope and He really wants to help you.

I wish I could tell you what the good witch told Dorothy in the *Wizard of Oz*: Just click your heels three times and say, "There's no place like home," but I haven't played with you up to this point and I won't start now. Clicking your heels won't get you there, no more than just wishing will. It takes *More* and the good news is that *More* is inside of you!

Where is it that you are trying to get to? I believe it is a place called healing, wholeness, and life. Jesus called it the abundant life. So how do you get there? Are you ready for the answer? LOOK! That's right, look. Not just anyplace though. You have to look in the right places or should I say in the right direction:

Look up. Not just to the heavens or the stars, although if you did they would speak volumes about the One who put them there and how He feels about you. I am suggesting that we must look to God. In the Old Testament after Israel had sinned, God punished them with a painful sickness. He had Moses shape a bronze serpent and put it on a stick before the congregation and all who looked on it were healed. That serpent was a type of Jesus Christ, and if you and I look to Him, there is healing for us as well:

- Our look must be focused. We must turn our gaze and expectation to Him.

- Our look must be in faith. We must believe as we look to Jesus that He will come to our aid and He will help us.

- Our look must be fixed. We must stay fixed on Him, and unlike Peter, no matter what is going on around us we must keep our eyes on him.

Look within. There are times this is scary. For some of us our problem is we have done this too much and too often. However, in this case, we must look within to discover several things and to make sure we are not harboring unforgiveness, bitterness, or hatred in our heart:

- We look within to make sure our heart is right: *"If I regard iniquity in my heart, the Lord will not hear me. . ."* (Psalm 66:18, KJV).

- We look within to find and release the faith that is resident inside us: *"For I say, through the grace given unto me, to every man that is among you, not to think of himself more highly than he ought to think; but to think soberly, according as God hath dealt to every man the measure of faith"* (Romans 12:3, KJV).

- We look within to find strength to go on, just like you found strength to begin this journey.

<u>Look around</u>. Again, let me caution you that sometimes our challenges have come because we looked at people rather than God. In this instance, I want to challenge you to look around you. For some of us this is difficult simply because we have been hurt and betrayed by people. But, I need you to believe that God has put people in your path and in your life that will love you, accept you, and help you. You just have to look for them.

I know that if you are willing to take these steps of faith, you will discover that God has put a road beneath your feet that will lead you to your healing and deliverance.

I have enjoyed taking this trip with you. Don't forget, they are singing our song and playing our music, so let's get on the floor and dance!

Please enjoy this excerpt from *Caution: God at Work: Trusting God through Tough Times*
ISBN 978-0-9764022-5-1.

From time to time every preacher finds themselves asking the age-old question of what shall I preach? The genesis of that question is not found in the scarcity of preaching material, but rather a desire on the part of the preacher to meet a real need in the life of the worshiper. The preacher's goal is for those who sit under their preaching to be confronted and comforted by the claims and promises of God.

I suppose in some ways those of us who preach the Gospel can find comfort in knowing that we are not the first to raise this question. In fact, the question is as old as the prophet Isaiah: *"A voice says, 'cry out.' And I said, 'What shall I cry?'"* (Isaiah 40:6), which only goes to show that even the prophet occasionally found himself stymied as to what he should preach. I have to confess that after preaching almost thirty-five years that every now and then I find myself wondering, "What can I say that I haven't already said?" and the answer came to me as I was rummaging through the Word of God.

All of us have seen those signs that read, "Caution: People at Work," which serve as a reminder for us to slow down, be more alert and aware because there are men and women on the road working. You may be upset that you have to slow down because they are working, but what you have to remember is that they are working for your good. I hate seeing the orange barrels because they usually mean that it is going to take longer for me to reach my destination. I have to slow down for a temporary inconvenience while people are working on a permanent improvement. Sometimes the road work is hidden behind a canopy and you can't see what is going on behind it. You must understand that while God may have you slowing down, and while you may not be making the progress that you want to make, you can still celebrate the fact that God is at work. And if God is working, He is always working for your good, even when you cannot see it.

Caution: God at Work is meant to bring hope to Christians who find themselves in difficult situations or dealing with some painful fact or reality in their life. This book is meant to remind you that no matter what you face, or what you go through, there is never a time when God is not at work in you and at work on your behalf. In fact, beloved, right now while you are hurting, right now while your heart is breaking, right now in the midst of your pain and your questions, God is at work.

Other Books by
Bishop Timothy J. Clarke

Caution: God at Work – Trusting God through tough times

Celebrating the Family: Lessons from the Book of Ruth

Living in the Blessed Place

Making the Most of Your Time

The Price of Victory: Strategies for winning a faith fight

Reclaim Your Spiritual Health

To My Sisters Beloved: A trilogy of encouragement

www.ingramcontent.com/pod-product-compliance
Lightning Source LLC
Chambersburg PA
CBHW050348280326
41933CB00010BA/1384